A CHILD'S BOOK OF

Sea Shells

by William M. Hutchinson

*august webb city, Fla.
1960*

Maxton Publishers, Inc.
New York

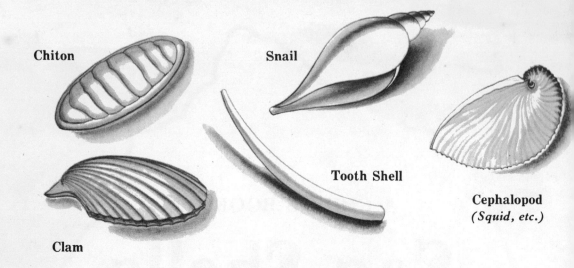

Chiton

Snail

Tooth Shell

Cephalopod
(*Squid, etc.*)

Clam

Homes in the Sea

Have you ever been to the seashore and found a sea shell lying on the beach where the waves left it? Probably the shell was empty, but before it was empty, it was the home of a wonderful little animal, which has a soft, unsegmented body, like a snail or an oyster. There are thousands of different kinds of these creatures. Each one has a remarkable organ called a mantle secreting the material from which it makes its shell.

All of these animals are called marine mollusks. There are five different groups, each producing a different kind of shell. The **Chitons** have shells with eight plates. The **Tooth Shells** are conical, curving, and open at both ends. The **Clams** are bivalves having two shells. The **Snails** have one spiral-like shell and are called univalves. The **Cephalopods** are animals like the Squid, the Octopus, and the Nautilus.

For protection, the mollusks build shells in which they live. To help conceal them, nature has patterned and colored their shells to look like their surroundings. They live in deep as well as shallow waters.

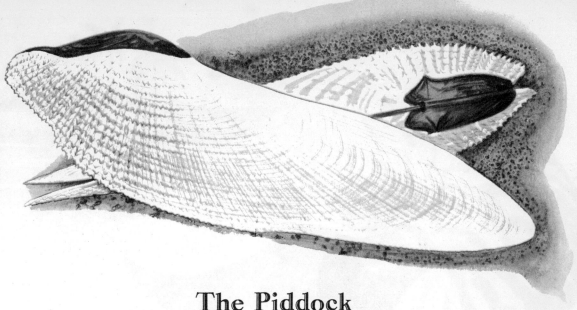

The Piddock

The Piddock is a boring clam which burrows into wood, coral, rock and clay, and is found the world over. The one pictured here is a stone-boring clam, the largest found on the English coasts.

The Piddock has a thin, brittle shell, which is covered with rows of small points, the largest toward the base of the shell. When it bores into soft stone, it uses its shell like a file, rocking back and forth, the points scraping away the stone. In this way, the Piddock digs out a home for itself which it never leaves. It sucks in its food and oxygen through its long syphons.

Because the Piddock is phosphorescent like a firefly, the rock piles where it lives glow with little points of light at night, especially during the warmer weather. The Piddock shell is white, marked with pinkish-brown and some yellow. It grows to be five or six inches long and is most abundant on the south coast of England in the deposits of chalk and soft stone.

The Nautilus

The poet, Oliver Wendell Holmes, wrote a famous poem about the Pearly or Chambered Nautilus. Found in the deep warm waters of the Pacific and Indian Oceans, the Nautilus is a mollusk like Squids and Argonauts.

The Nautilus starts life with a shell of a single chamber, but as it grows, it adds other chambers, each one larger than the one before. As it enlarges into a spiral formation, it keeps moving into the new chamber and seals off the one behind it. Sometimes, a large shell may have as many as thirty chambers.

The Nautilus floats about hanging head downward. Around its mouth, it has about 100 small tentacles or arms with which it catches its food — crabs and other animals. For protection, it can withdraw completely into its shell.

The small picture below shows a Nautilus shell cut in half so you can see the chambers inside.

The Scorpion Shell

Many soldiers and sailors, who served in the South Pacific islands during World War II, would recognize this shell. It is easily identified because of its odd shape.

There are 10 species. A fully-developed scorpion has six hooks or points projecting from the body of the shell. These make it look something like the real, live scorpion.

When found on the beach, many Scorpion shells are damaged. The action of the waves tumbling the shells about as they carry them ashore, wear down and break off the points.

This shell is thick and heavy, striped like a Zebra on the lips, with yellow and orange on the underside of the hooks. The surface of an undamaged shell resembles porcelain.

Volutes

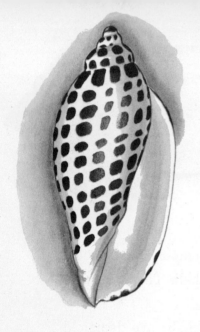

Volutes are favorites with shell collectors because of their colorful and unusual patterns. More or less vase-shaped, they occur with many different kinds of ornamentations. The spire is always prominent. Handsome, graceful and good-sized, there are many rare and valuable species, which are highly prized.

Found in warm and tropic seas, Volutes live on rocks and coral ledges in deep water. They are not often found on beaches.

The one shown above, Juno's Volute, a valuable species, is found off the east and west coasts of Florida. It is pinkish white with brown spots and the inside is salmon pink. Some have a creamy surface decorated by squarish orange spots in spiral rows. Juno's Volute is a prize for any collection.

The volutes shown below are all from the Pacific Ocean around Australia.

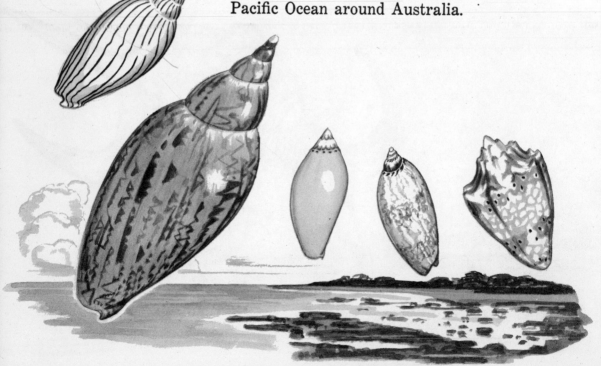

Bay Scallop

Scallops

At least 200 species of Scallops live in
seas all around the world. Scallops are
bivalves, but instead of crawling like
most clams, they skitter about in a
jerky, zigzag fashion by rapidly opening and closing their valves.
Scallops are a favorite sea-food. The single muscle of the Scallop
makes movement possible and is the edible part.

The Bay Scallop, which lives in shallow water, is dredged by the
ton and sold in a wide market.

The Callico Scallop is numerous on beaches from North Carolina
to Cuba. Thousands upon thousands are used each year to make
different kinds of shell novelties, especially ash trays. These shells
come in wide varieties of patterns and colors, such as mottled
white, pink, yellow-orange, purple and brown.

The Lion's Paw is another collector's item. Its rich red coloring
and knobby surface make it rather handsome.

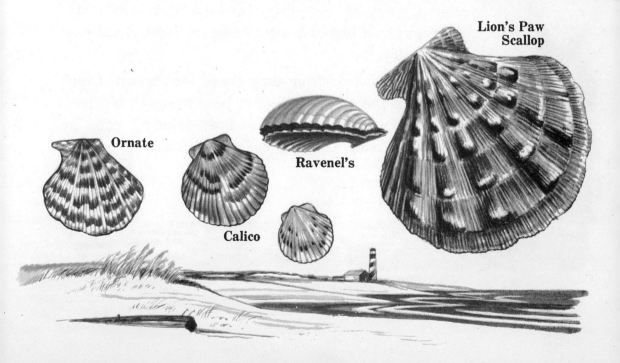

Lion's Paw
Scallop

Ornate

Ravenel's

Calico

Turban Shell

Turban Shells are found living in tropical seas in all parts of the world. Usually shaped like a turban, they are solid and heavy and have smooth, knobby or spiny surfaces, which are brightly colored. Most Turban Shells have an iridescent pearly undercoat.

They also have what is called an operculum or door to close their shells. Many marine snails have doors which are carried on the outside when the snail moves about, as shown in the drawing at the left. When the snail retires into its shell, the door is pulled in, sealing the shell.

A famous shell of this door-bearing group is a Turban Shell (shown above) from the rocks and reefs of the South Pacific. Its brightly-colored, jewel-like operculum is called a "Cat's-eye" and it may be green, blue or brown. These are polished and used in jewelry.

In Scandinavia, from early times, the Turban-shaped Shells of the green snail have been mounted in silver, studded with gems and used as drinking cups by royalty. Today, they are collectors' items.

Abalone

The Abalone is valued for its beauty and for its usefulness. The inside of this shell has a lustrous, pearly surface and is used for jewelry, buttons and souvenirs. The exterior is made into mantel and cabinet ornaments.

Many tons of these shells are utilized to make breakwaters in harbors. Abalones also serve as food, and commercial fishermen catch them for this purpose.

In its native habitat, the Abalone clamps itself to rocks with its shell uppermost. It breathes by extracting oxygen from water taken in under the shell and pumped out through a row of holes on one of its sides.

The Abalone is plentiful on the Pacific coast of the United States and are also found on the shores of Japan, Australia, and the Channel Islands off the coast of France.

The Argonaut

Of the same family as the Nautilus, the Argonaut, or Paper Nautilus as it is sometimes called, is another cephalopod which is widely distributed in tropical and warm seas.

It is found in the Mediterranean Sea, in waters off Northern Australia, Florida, Pacific Islands, the Cape of Good Hope and in the Gulf of California.

The Argonaut, a kind of octopus, has eight long arms. From two of the arms expanded into thin membranes, the female Argonaut produces a delicate, paper-thin shell, which is really an egg case.

The pictures below show the Argonaut with the egg case, the eggs in the case, and views of the translucent, milky white shell.

The Chitons

The Chitons, or Coat-of-Mail Shells, are primitive forms of mollusks and are thought to be little different from their ancestors, which lived thousands of years ago. Their shells, divided into eight overlapping plates or sections, look like a coat of armor.

Most Chitons live along shores under stones, where the bottom is muddy and in the area between high and low tide levels. The Chiton fastens itself to a rock and if pulled loose, it will roll itself up into a ball like an Armadillo, completely protected by its armor and stay that way until left undisturbed.

These strange little animals do not like sunshine and gather at night in large numbers where seaweed is decaying. They occur in many different colors and a variety of odd patterns.

These shown here are from the coast of Mexico. But they are also found in warm waters in other parts of the world.

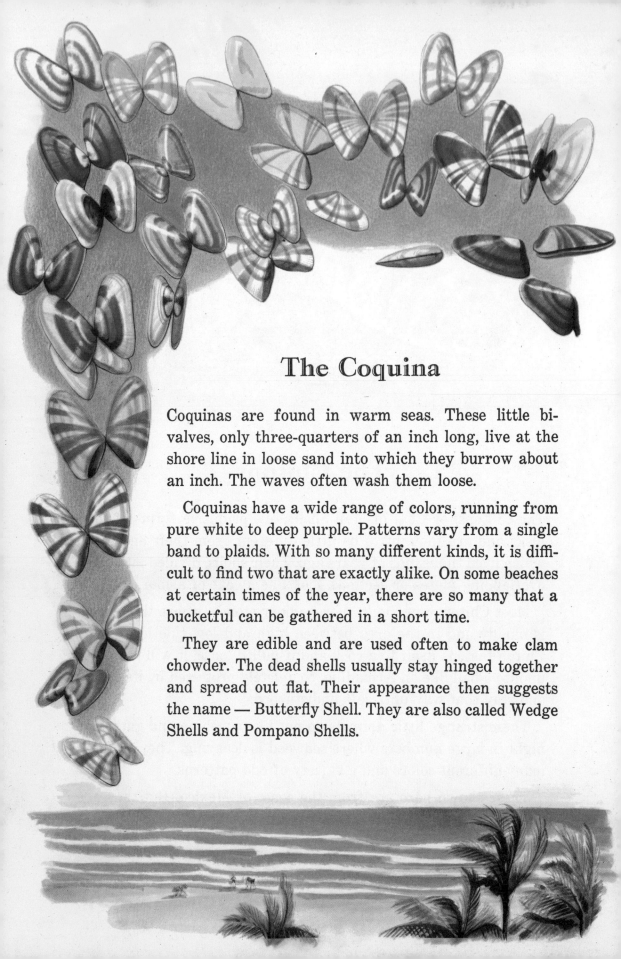

The Coquina

Coquinas are found in warm seas. These little bivalves, only three-quarters of an inch long, live at the shore line in loose sand into which they burrow about an inch. The waves often wash them loose.

Coquinas have a wide range of colors, running from pure white to deep purple. Patterns vary from a single band to plaids. With so many different kinds, it is difficult to find two that are exactly alike. On some beaches at certain times of the year, there are so many that a bucketful can be gathered in a short time.

They are edible and are used often to make clam chowder. The dead shells usually stay hinged together and spread out flat. Their appearance then suggests the name — Butterfly Shell. They are also called Wedge Shells and Pompano Shells.

Knobbed Pear Conch

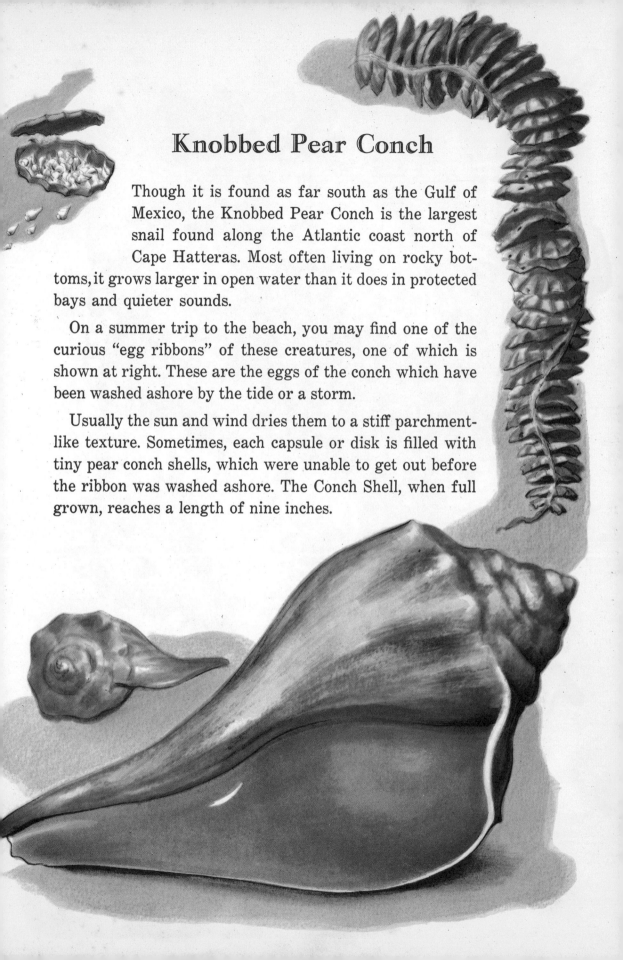

Though it is found as far south as the Gulf of Mexico, the Knobbed Pear Conch is the largest snail found along the Atlantic coast north of Cape Hatteras. Most often living on rocky bottoms, it grows larger in open water than it does in protected bays and quieter sounds.

On a summer trip to the beach, you may find one of the curious "egg ribbons" of these creatures, one of which is shown at right. These are the eggs of the conch which have been washed ashore by the tide or a storm.

Usually the sun and wind dries them to a stiff parchment-like texture. Sometimes, each capsule or disk is filled with tiny pear conch shells, which were unable to get out before the ribbon was washed ashore. The Conch Shell, when full grown, reaches a length of nine inches.

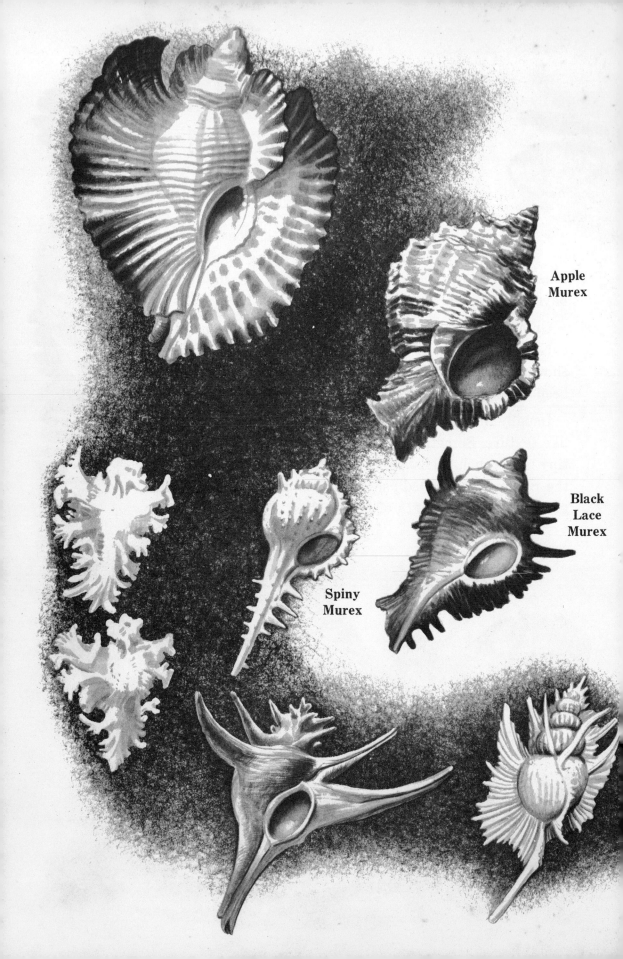

Apple
Murex

Black
Lace
Murex

Spiny
Murex

The Murex Shells

Different types of these rock shells are found all over the world. However, they are most plentiful in the tropics. They can be recognized usually by their spine-covered surfaces. Mostly they live on rocky, gravelly bottoms where they feed on other mollusks.

Venus's Comb is one of the most unique members in the Murex family, all of which have unusual shapes. It comes from the Pacific Ocean, but there are some of this group in the Indian Ocean, too. The Apple, Spiny, and Black Lace Murex are all found around the Gulf of Mexico.

The Spiny Murex is the largest, growing to three inches in length. The other shells shown are from the Pacific.

Murex shells have special glands which secrete a bluish-red dye. The famous Tyrian Purple, a dye used by the ancient Romans, was made from two different Murex shells found in the Mediterranean. Making the dye and the dyeing of cloth was then a thriving industry.

Venus Comb

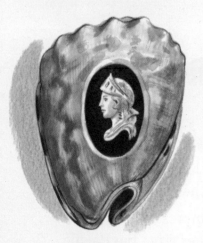

Helmet Shells

Some of these shells are ten inches long, while some smaller members are only three inches in length. They are easily recognized by their three-cornered shape and the large, thick lips at the opening.

These shells are used to make cameos, ornaments and other jewelry. To make a cameo, the outer shell layer is carved and cut through to the undercoating, as shown in the small picture above. At one time these shells were commercially in great demand because of the popularity of cameos.

The finest cameos are those made from the Red Helmet of the Mediterranean and the Red Sea. Two found on the southern coast of the Western Hemisphere, the King or Sardonyx Helmet, below left, and the Yellow Helmet, sometimes called Queen Helmet, right, also make beautiful cameos.

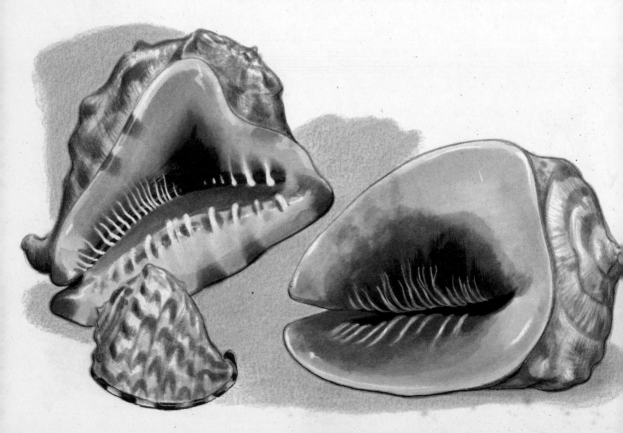

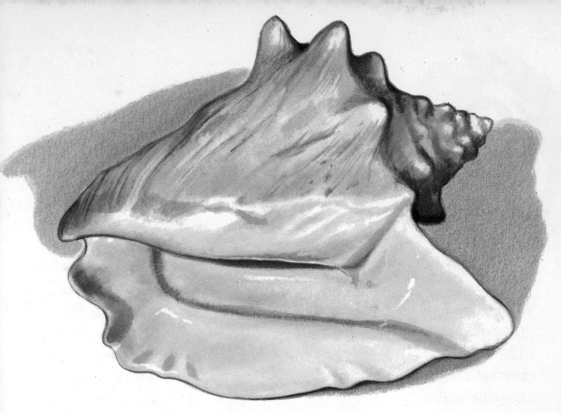

Giant Conch

You have probably seen the Giant Conch, or Queen Conch, used as a doorstop or garden decoration. It is about a foot long and sometimes weighs as much as 5 pounds. The Giant Conch is a scavenger living on dead fish and other carrion.

They are energetic creatures and hop about on the sea floor of their habitat. When frightened, they take great, long leaps.

Semi-precious pearls are sometimes found in this conch. Natives of the West Indies once used the shell to make tools. The Giant Conch is now exported from the Bahama Islands in large numbers for the making of porcelain and commercial cameos. Huge quantities are shipped to Liverpool and other porcelain-manufacturing centers of the world.

In the West Indies the flesh is eaten in salads and chowder.

The Wentletraps

The Precious Wentletrap

Graceful little shells, the Wentletraps are distributed widely throughout the world. They are also called Staircase Shells because they closely resemble spiral staircases.

The Precious Wentletrap is the most famous of the family. This pure white shell was at one time in such demand by shell collectors that fabulous prices were paid for specimens. It lives in Asiatic waters. The Chinese made imitation ones of rice paste, which were so perfect they fooled unsuspecting Europeans, who bought them as genuine shells.

Shown about twice enlarged, all the shells below are found on the Atlantic Coast of the United States, except the Ladder Shell. This one likes extremely cold water and lives in the Greenland coast area. Off the Grand Banks of southeastern Newfoundland, Ladder Shells occur abundantly in the stomachs of fishes.

Nearly all Wentletraps are white but there are also many in various colors. All have interesting and delicate structures and are highly valued by shell collectors.

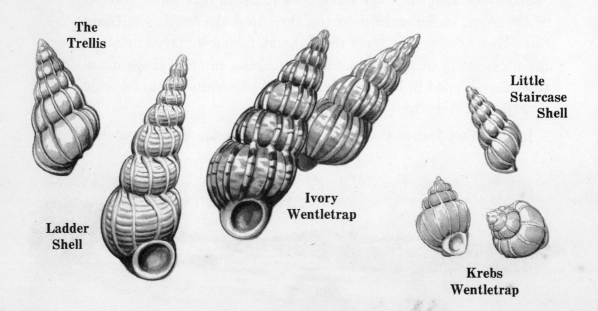

The Trellis

Little Staircase Shell

Ivory Wentletrap

Ladder Shell

Krebs Wentletrap

Sundial

The outer spiral of the Sundial Shell is marked with brown spots which make it look something like the Sundial from which it gets its name. The base is usually purplish on white. It is found in shallow waters from North Carolina to the West Indies. A much larger species lives in the Indian and Pacific Oceans.

The Music Volute

Its pattern, spotted lines suggesting bars and notes of written music, gives the Music Volute its apt name. These fine brown lines and spots are on a creamy flesh ground color. They range from two to four inches in length, and are solid and stout in structure. The Music Volute lives in deep water around the Island of Trinidad.

King's Crown Conch

This shell has a pretty banded pattern in bluish white, chocolate brown, amber and mixtures of these colors. On its shoulders and at its base, it has a row of spines which are fragile and easily broken. Often the color is spoiled by a marine growth on the shell.

The Crown Conch is a fierce snail which preys on other snails and bivalves. It does not hesitate to attack them even though they are larger than itself. Only a few other mollusks can over-power it in its own habitat.

Five inches is a normal adult size for the Crown Conch. It is found in brackish water off the South Atlantic coast of the United States.

Triton's Trumpet

From the Indian Ocean, the waters around Japan, and the Philippine Islands comes Triton's Trumpet, with a slightly different variety found in the Caribbean and the Gulf of Mexico.

A richly-decorated and handsome shell, it has patterns that resemble the plumage of certain pheasants. A foot-and-a-half long when fully grown, it is a stout, heavy shell, the largest of the group of Triton shells.

In ancient Greek mythology, the sea god Triton used a shell of this family as a trumpet. It is still used as a trumpet by some Pacific Island tribes and also serves as a teakettle and water vessel in some localities. It is a colorful addition to any collection.

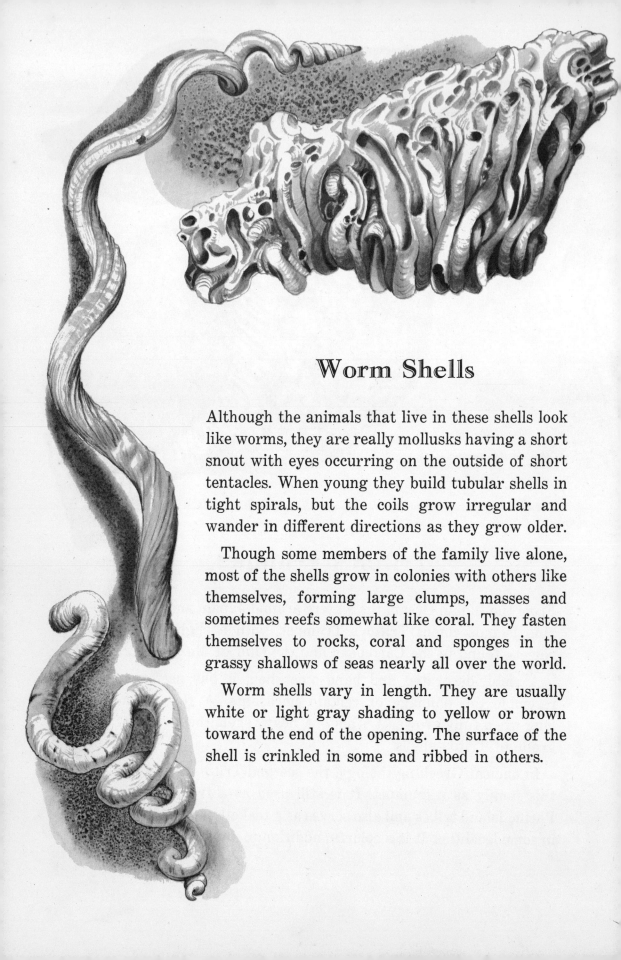

Worm Shells

Although the animals that live in these shells look like worms, they are really mollusks having a short snout with eyes occurring on the outside of short tentacles. When young they build tubular shells in tight spirals, but the coils grow irregular and wander in different directions as they grow older.

Though some members of the family live alone, most of the shells grow in colonies with others like themselves, forming large clumps, masses and sometimes reefs somewhat like coral. They fasten themselves to rocks, coral and sponges in the grassy shallows of seas nearly all over the world.

Worm shells vary in length. They are usually white or light gray shading to yellow or brown toward the end of the opening. The surface of the shell is crinkled in some and ribbed in others.

Terebra Shells

The snails that live in the Terebra or Auger Shells are a curious sight crawling about with their long, tapering shells towering over them like steeples.

They are found in warm tropical seas and some of these snails are poisonous.

These Terebras are found usually in shallow water on sand bars and flats. They vary in color from ashy gray to pale brown, but have the same general shape, tapering with many whorls.

There is a spotted Auger Shell found in the South Sea Islands which Polynesians shape into chisels.

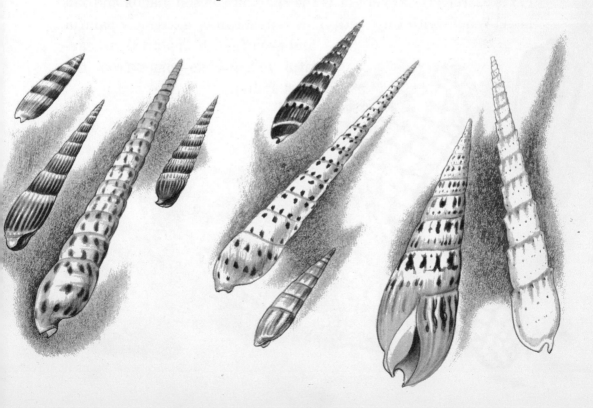

Cone Shells

Great variety of colors and patterns make the Cone Shells famous in the shell world. They prefer living in warm waters. Those found in the Pacific and Indian Oceans are dangerous because the snails have a poisonous bite.

The Florida Cone (1), the little Mouse Cone (2), and the Cloudy Cone (3) are all found in Florida waters. The largest cone found on the Atlantic Coast is the Alphabet Cone (4) which gets its name from its pattern resembling Chinese letters. Unusual in color and pattern is a Japanese Cone (5).

From the Philippines come two handsome cones (6 and 7), but (7) is extremely dangerous as the snail has poison glands and can inject venom with tiny teeth. This venom can be extremely painful and even fatal to man. (8) A beautiful yellow cone comes from the East Indies.

The Cowries

The tropic seas all around the world have Cowry Shells, always highly valued by collectors. They have shiny, porcelain-like surfaces with an endless variety of color and pattern. The mantle of this mollusk usually spreads around the shell completely and is often brilliantly-colored. Cowries have been used as money and ornaments by primitive people in all parts of the tropics.

The Measled Cowry (1), Gray Cowry (2), and Little Yellow Cowry (3) are all found in Florida; the last of this group being also found in some European waters. The others, 4, 5, 6, and 7, are found in the Pacific Ocean and fairly often on the reefs of New Guinea, the Philippines and other islands. Of these, the Golden Cowry (6) is the most precious. It comes from the Fiji Islands, where it is a symbol of authority, the property of chiefs, and worn as a crown.

Pelican's Foot

At the low-tide mark, around the European coasts, there is found a curiously-shaped shell, resembling a pelican's foot in appearance.

When young, the Pelican's Foot has a conical spire shape. Not until it is full-grown, do the peculiar flaring lip formations develop, which make it so unusual. It has a yellowish-white color, stained with brown, making it look much like the sand over which it crawls in its search for food. Mollusks of this species are slow and awkward when they move. This strange-looking animal is about two inches long.

A smaller shell of the same family, the Shetland Pelican's Foot, is found only off the Shetland Islands in deep water.

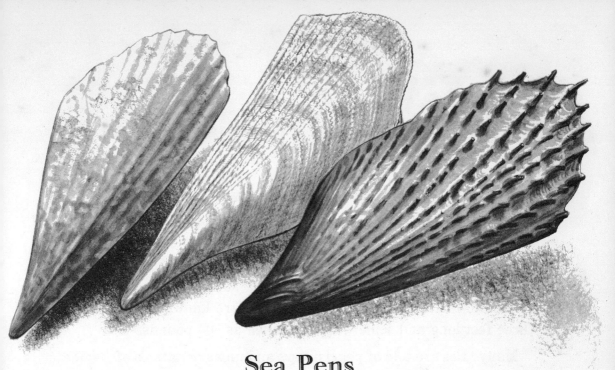

Sea Pens

Sea Pen Shells are large wedge-shaped bivalves, some growing to more than two feet long. The shells are thin and fragile and some are transparent. Usually they live in mud or sand, or among rocks of warm seas.

These bivalves spin silky strands of thread, by which they anchor themselves to rocks. This anchor is called a byssus. From the byssus of the Mediterranean Pen Shell, men gather these fine threads and weave them into a very soft cloth. It has a metallic sheen and articles such as gloves are made from this beautiful fabric.

Shown above, from the left, they are the orange-yellow Flesh Pen, the olive-brown Sawtooth Pen, and the brownish-black Stiff Pen Shell.

The Giant Clam

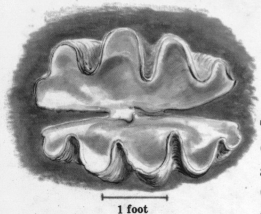

1 foot

The largest of all shells is the Giant Clam which lives in the Pacific Ocean and tropic seas. When young, the Giant Clam settles itself on some spot in a coral reef and allows the coral to grow all around it so that it becomes imbedded in the reef. These monster shells are known to grow over three feet long and some weigh as much as 500 pounds.

Many tales are told of pearl divers and unwary natives of Pacific Islands having a hand or foot trapped between the valves in the tremendously powerful grip of the clam and being drowned. By cutting the large hinge muscle with a knife, the clam can be made powerless to close its valves.

Pacific natives enjoy eating this muscle raw. The rest of the clam is eaten as chowder. The Giant Clam has a beautiful peacock-colored mantle which can be seen when the valves are open. The shell is white, the interior smooth, the outside ridged and covered with marine growths.

These enormous shells are used as baptismal fonts in churches, ornaments in gardens, and even as fish pools and punch bowls.

In the Caroline Islands, east of the Philippines, natives chisel axe heads out of the thickest parts.